Recipes by Mary Ward

Modern Publishing
A Division of Unisystems, Inc.
New York, New York 10022

Printed in Canada

INTRODUCTION

Convenient Cooking™ is just what the modern cook ordered for quick, easy and delicious food.

Whether you are preparing a simple meal for one, an intimate dinner for two, or a banquet for family or friends, the Convenient Cooking™ series will take the work out of planning and preparing your menus, enabling you to enjoy the occasion and the food!

Eight exciting titles provide a convenient recipe center of easy-to-handle, easy-to-read books for every cooking need: meats and ground meats; seafood; chicken and poultry; soups, salads and sauces; omelettes, casseroles and vegetables; microwave meals; desserts; and Cajun food.

Whether you are a beginning cook, or a seasoned food preparer, you will delight in choosing from the range of basic, traditional fare to exotic meals that this series has to offer.

Welcome to the enjoyable and delicious world of **Convenient Cooking.**™

Notes:

* All recipes in this book should be prepared in/with microwave proof cookware.

**When recipes in this book call for covering cookware, cover—loosely, unless otherwise noted—with plastic wrap or wax paper.

***These recipes were tested in a 600 watt microwave oven which will heat 1 cup of cold water to boiling point in 2 1/2 minutes.

ALBONDIGAS (MEXICAN STYLE MEATBALLS)

Ingredients:

1 pound ground chicken
or turkey
1 egg
1/4 cup chopped
cilantro (available in
most supermarket
produce departments,
or use parsley)
1 medium-sized onion,
chopped
2 cloves garlic, minced
2 fresh or canned
jalapeno peppers,
medium or hot
1 teaspoon salt
1/2 teaspoon cumin
2 large tomatoes
1 (4 ounce) can diced
green chillis
1/2 cup chopped
cilantro
1 teaspoon salt

Directions:

Combine ground chicken, egg, 1/4 cup cilantro, onion, garlic, 2 jalapeno peppers, salt and cumin. Mix with hands until mixture holds together well. Form into 2 to 3 dozen meatballs. Place meatballs on a microwavable tray, and microwave on high for 10 to 12 minutes or until meatballs are cooked and firm. Turn tray frequently. Remove meatballs to a serving platter, discarding fat. Meanwhile, in a blender cup or food processor, blend tomatoes, canned chillis, 1/2 cup cilantro and salt until very smooth. Place in a 2-cup glass mixing bowl and microwave on high for 3 minutes, just until hot. Spoon this hot salsa over meatballs and serve immediately.

Serves: Makes 2 to 3 dozen meatballs.

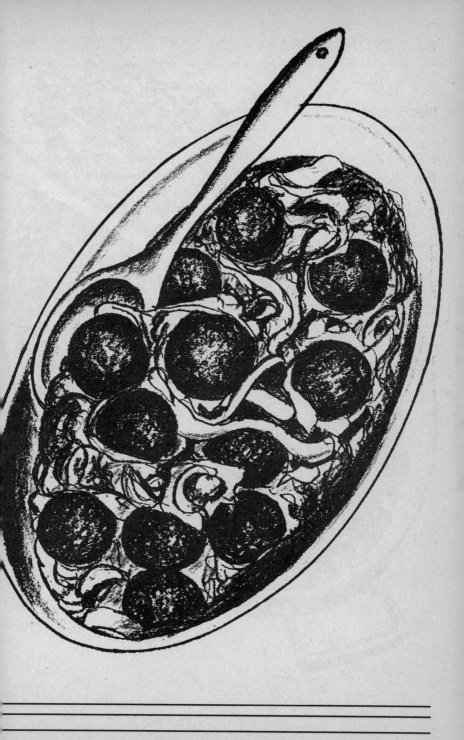

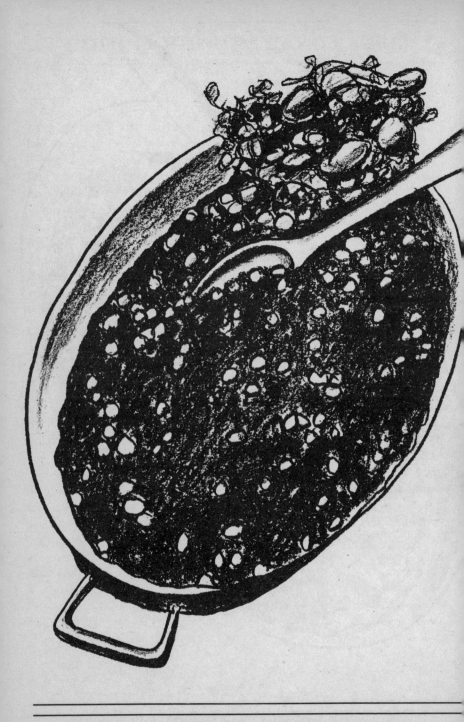

CHILLI CON QUESO WITH CHORIZO

Ingredients:

8 ounces chorizo sausage (available at many supermarket meat counters, or use hot Italian sausage)

1 small onion, chopped

2 tablespoons green pepper

1/2 cup processed cheese with jalapeno peppers

2 tablespoons milk

Corn chips, nachos, toasted tortillas

Directions:

Remove casing from sausage. Crumble meat into a 9-inch glass pie plate. Add onion and green pepper. Microwave on high for 3 to 5 minutes, until sausage is cooked and vegetables are tender. Remove sausage and vegetables with a slotted spoon to a clean, 2-cup, microwave serving dish. Discard sausage fat. Grate cheese and fold into sausage mixture. Sprinkle with milk. Microwave for 2 minutes or until cheese is melted and blended with meat and vegetables. Serve hot with corn chips, nachos, or toasted tortillas.

Serves: Makes 1 1/2 cups.

HAM 'N' EGG

Ingredients:

1 cup smoked ham, chopped

1 small green pepper, chopped

1 small onion, chopped

1 small, ripe tomato, chopped

2 tablespoons butter

4 large eggs, whipped with a fork

4 slices whole wheat bread, toasted

Chilli sauce, salsa, or catsup

Directions:

Place ham, green pepper, onion, tomato and butter in a 9-inch glass pie plate. Microwave on high for 2 to 3 minutes, until vegetables are tender. Carefully whisk eggs into this mixture. Microwave for 1 1/2 to 2 minutes until eggs are almost set. Allow mixture to rest for 5 minutes before cutting. Cut into wedges and serve atop toast with chilli sauce, salsa, or catsup on the side.

Serves: 4

ARTICHOKE NIBBLES

Ingredients:
1/2 cup mayonnaise
1 teaspoon Dijon
  mustard
1 tablespoon prepared
  horseradish
1/4 cup sour cream
1/2 cup Romano
  cheese, grated
2 (14 ounce) cans
  water-packed
  artichoke hearts
2 tablespoons butter
1/2 cup fresh bread
  crumbs

Directions:
Blend together mayonnaise, mustard, horseradish, sour cream, and Romano cheese. Drain and rinse artichoke hearts. Pat dry between paper towels. Cut artichoke hearts into bite-sized pieces. Blend artichoke heart pieces with mayonnaise sauce and turn into a large glass pie plate. Place butter in a small glass bowl and microwave on high for 30 seconds. Toss bread with melted butter to coat. Sprinkle crumbs over artichoke mixture. Microwave on high for 2 to 4 minutes, turning occasionally, until cheese is melted. Serve immediately with toothpicks.

Serves: 8

CHEESE WINGS

Ingredients:
15 chicken wings (about
  2 1/2 to 3 pounds)
1/4 cup butter
1 cup seasoned bread
  crumbs
1/4 cup Provolone
  cheese, finely grated
1/4 cup Parmesan
  cheese, freshly grated
2 teaspoons chopped
  fresh parsley
1 teaspoon garlic salt
1/2 teaspoon paprika
1/2 teaspoon freshly
  ground pepper

Directions:
To prepare chicken wings: cut off wing tips and discard. Separate chicken wings at joints. You will have 30 wing pieces. Wash and pat dry. In a glass pie plate, melt butter on high for 30 seconds. Dip chicken wing pieces in melted butter, coating well. Combine bread crumbs, Provolone cheese, Parmesan cheese, fresh parsley, garlic salt, paprika, and freshly ground pepper in a shallow bowl. Dip chicken wing pieces in mixture and place on a large microwave tray. Place thicker parts of chicken wings on outside edges of tray. Microwave on high for 13 to 15 minutes.

Serves: 8

FRESH CHICKEN LIVER PATÉ

Ingredients:

2 large onions, chopped
2 cloves garlic, minced
1/4 cup olive oil
1 pound fresh chicken livers
1 teaspoon salt
1 teaspoon white pepper
2 tablespoons freshly chopped parsley
1 hard-cooked egg, finely chopped

Directions:

In a glass mixing bowl, combine onions, garlic and olive oil. Microwave on high for 6 to 8 minutes until vegetables are cooked. Wash chicken livers, removing any tough parts. Arrange chicken livers in a single layer in a 9-inch glass pie plate. Cover with a paper towel and microwave at medium until just cooked, about 5 minutes. Interior of chicken livers will be pink and hot. Do not overcook. Drain chicken livers and place in food processor or food grinder. Add onions, garlic, salt and pepper and grind or puree until smooth. Spoon into a decorative 3-cup bowl; garnish with chopped parsley and hard-cooked egg.

Serves: Makes 3 cups.

HOT DOGS

Ingredients:

1 cup homestyle gravy (homemade or canned)
1/2 cup currant jelly
2 tablespoons chilli sauce
1 tablespoon prepared horseradish
1 pound turkey franks

Directions:

Combine gravy with jelly, chilli sauce, and horseradish in a microwave dish. Cut turkey franks into 1-inch slices. Add to gravy sauce. Heat on high for 5 to 7 minutes, until sauce bubbles and franks are heated through. Serve with toothpicks.

Serves: 10

HOT CRABS

Ingredients:
3 tablespoons flour
3 tablespoons butter
1 cup milk
7 to 8 ounces fresh, frozen or canned crab meat (or crab meat-like product)
1 tablespoon pimiento, minced
2 tablespoons chopped green pepper
1/2 teaspoon salt
1/2 cup Romano cheese, shredded
6 toasted English muffin halves (3 whole muffins)
Paprika
Mint or parsley sprigs

Directions:
In a 2-cup microwave-proof dish, microwave flour with butter for 1 minute. Whisk in milk, and microwave for 30 seconds longer. Whisk to remove any lumps; sauce should be smooth and thick. Drain crab meat and add to white sauce with pimiento, green pepper, salt and Romano cheese. Blend well. Place toasted English muffin halves on a microwave tray. Divide crab meat filling into 6 portions and place on muffins. Microwave on high for 3 minutes or until cheese melts. Garnish with paprika and parsley or mint sprigs.

Serves: 6

NACHOS

Ingredients:
6 jalapeno peppers
4 cups nacho chips
1 cup processed cheese with jalapeno peppers, grated

Directions:
Stem and seed jalapeno peppers. Slice into 48 slices (8 slices per pepper). After slicing jalapenos, wash hands thoroughly to remove hot jalapeno oil from hands. On a microwave tray, place nacho chips. Top with grated cheese. Top each nacho with a jalapeno pepper ring. Microwave on high for 2 to 3 minutes, until all cheese is melted.

Serves: 4

HOT 'N' SPICY CLAM DIP

Ingredients:
- 1 (8 ounce) package cream cheese
- 2 tablespoons chopped pimiento
- 2 tablespoons chopped green pepper
- 1 tablespoon minced onion
- 1 clove garlic, minced
- 1 tablespoon prepared horseradish
- 1/2 teaspoon salt
- 1/2 teaspoon freshly ground pepper
- 1 teaspoon Worcestershire sauce
- 2 tablespoons milk
- 1 (8 ounce) can minced clams
- Parsley sprigs
- Crackers
- Vegetable crudité

Directions:
Place cream cheese in a medium-sized microwave bowl. Microwave on medium for 30 seconds until softened. Blend softened cream cheese with pimiento, green pepper, onion, garlic, horseradish, salt, pepper, Worcestershire and milk. Drain and rinse clams. Fold into cream cheese mixture. Refrigerate. When ready to serve, place in a microwave decorative bowl and microwave on high for 2 to 2 and 1/2 minutes, until mixture is hot. Garnish with parsley sprigs; serve with crackers and vegetable crudité.

Serves: Makes 2 1/2 cups dip.

HOT PEPPERY CREAM CHEESE DIP

Ingredients:
1 (8 ounce) package
   cream cheese
1/2 cup hot pepper
   cheese (Monterey
   Jack)
1/2 cup mayonnaise
1 small onion, grated
1 teaspoon hot pepper
   sauce
1 teaspoon
   Worcestershire sauce
2 tablespoons chopped
   chives
1 tablespoon chopped
   pimiento

Directions:
Place cream cheese in a 1-quart glass bowl. Microwave on medium for 2 minutes to soften cheese. Stir in hot pepper cheese, mayonnaise, onion, hot pepper sauce, Worcestershire sauce, chives, and pimiento. Refrigerate until serving time. When ready to serve, place in 3-cup microwave serving bowl and microwave on medium for 4 to 5 minutes until dip is warm and hot pepper cheese is melting. This dip is good with crudité, as well as with crackers and corn chips.

Serves: Makes 2 cups.

HOT SALMON SANDWICHES WITH FOUR CHEESES

Ingredients:
2 packages cocktail rye
   bread
1 (15 ounce) can
   salmon
1 (8 ounce) package
   cream cheese
1/2 cup Cheddar
   cheese, grated
1/2 cup Parmesan
   cheese, freshly grated
1/2 cup farmer's cheese,
   grated
1 teaspoon salt
1/2 teaspoon paprika

Directions:
Toast cocktail rye slices until evenly browned. Drain salmon. In a 1-quart glass bowl, combine salmon with cream cheese. Heat on high for 1 minute until cream cheese softens and blends with salmon. To salmon mixture, add Cheddar cheese, Parmesan cheese, and farmer's cheese. Blend in salt and paprika. Place toast slices on a microwave tray. Spread mixture on toasted cocktail rye and microwave in batches. One dozen salmon sandwiches will take about 2 minutes to heat in microwave on high. Serve hot.

Serves: Makes 4 dozen sandwiches.

IDAHOS WITH HERBS

Ingredients:

2 large Idaho potatoes
1/4 cup butter
1/4 cup freshly grated
Parmesan cheese
1/2 cup finely crushed
cheese crackers
1 teaspoon garlic
powder
1/4 cup finely chopped,
fresh basil (or 2
tablespoons dry basil)
2 tablespoons finely
chopped, fresh
tarragon (or 1
tablespoon dry
tarragon)
1/2 teaspoon paprika
1 teaspoon salt
1 tablespoon grated
Parmesan cheese
Tarragon sprigs

Directions:

Scrub potatoes with vegetable brush to remove any surface dirt and blemishes. Slice into 1/2-inch slices, wash, and pat dry. Microwave butter in a 9-inch, glass pie plate on high for 30 seconds. Coat potatoes with melted butter. Reserve any remaining butter. In a paper or plastic bag, blend 1/4 cup Parmesan cheese with cheese crackers, garlic powder, basil, tarragon, paprika and salt. Shake to insure proper blending of ingredients. Add potatoes to bag in batches, shaking to coat evenly. Place potato slices in a single layer on a large microwave tray. Drizzle with reserved butter. Cover with plastic wrap and microwave on high for 5 minutes, until potatoes are tender. Remove to a serving tray, sprinkle with 1 tablespoon Parmesan cheese, and garnish with tarragon sprigs.

Serves: 6

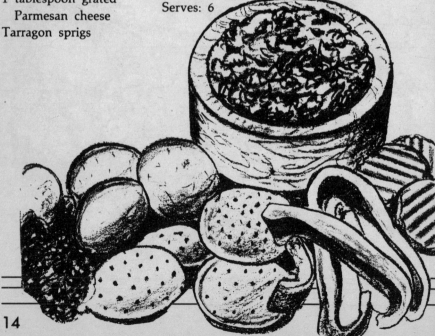

SPINACH BACON DIP

Ingredients:
2 slices bacon
1 (10 ounce) package frozen chopped spinach
1 cup sour cream
1/2 cup minced fresh parsley
4 green onions, chopped with tops
1 (4 ounce) can water chestnuts, chopped
1/2 cup mayonnaise
Juice of 1 lemon
1 teaspoon fresh dill (or 1 teaspoon dried dill)
1 teaspoon salt
Freshly ground pepper

Directions:
Place bacon on a microwave bacon rack. Cover with paper towel and microwave on high for 2 minutes, until bacon crisps. Drain and crumble bacon. Place unopened package of spinach on a microwave plate. (Remove any foil wrapping from package before placing in microwave.) Cook on high for 5 minutes. Remove spinach from package and drain thoroughly. Make sure all water is squeezed from spinach. In a medium-sized, glass mixing bowl, blend spinach with sour cream, parsley, onion, water chestnuts, mayonnaise, lemon, dill, salt and pepper. Fold in crumbled bacon. Refrigerate until ready to serve. This dip may be served cold, or you may heat it for 2 minutes on high for a hot spinach dip.

Serves: 16

ORANGE HONEY WHISKEY CHICKEN

Ingredients:
2 boneless, skinless, whole chicken breasts (1 1/2 pounds)
2 tablespoons honey
2 tablespoons cornstarch
1/2 cup orange marmalade
1/2 cup orange juice
1/2 cup whiskey
2 cups hot cooked rice

Directions:
Cut chicken into 4 serving pieces. Place in a 2-quart microwave casserole. Blend together honey, cornstarch, marmalade, orange juice and whiskey. Pour over chicken. Cover and microwave on high for 12 minutes. Turn, stir chicken, and microwave for 8 more minutes until chicken is tender. Serve immediately with hot, cooked rice.

Serves: 4

MAHOGANY WINGS

Ingredients:
- 2 pounds chicken wings (8 to 10 wings)
- 2 tablespoons teriyaki sauce
- 1/2 cup plum sauce (available in Oriental food departments and in some supermarkets)
- 2 tablespoons brown sugar
- 1 tablespoon Worcestershire sauce
- 1 clove garlic
- 1 slice ginger, minced
- 1 tablespoon arrowroot
- 2 tablespoons water

Directions:
Cut off wing tips and discard. Separate wings at joint. Wash and pat dry. Arrange wings, thickest parts to the outside, in a shallow, glass dish. Microwave on high for 5 to 6 minutes. Discard fat from dish. In a 1-quart glass bowl, combine teriyaki sauce, plum sauce, brown sugar, Worcestershire sauce, garlic, and ginger. Cover with plastic wrap and microwave on high for 2 minutes. Mix arrowroot with water and whisk into plum mixture. Cover and microwave 1 more minute; mahogany sauce should be thick and smooth. Pour mahogany sauce over chicken wings, cover with plastic, and microwave for 5 to 7 more minutes, until chicken wings are cooked and tender. Serve wings on a plate with a little sauce.

Serves: 4 to 6

STUFFED MUSHROOMS, ITALIAN STYLE

Ingredients:
24 large mushrooms
1 pound hot Italian sausage
2 cloves garlic, minced
1/2 cup fine dry bread crumbs
1/4 cup Romano cheese, grated
2 tablespoons fresh tarragon, chopped (or 1 tablespoon dry tarragon)
2 tablespoons fresh basil, chopped (or 1 tablespoon dried basil)

Directions:
Wash and stem mushrooms. Place mushrooms on a large microwave tray and set aside. Chop mushroom stems. Remove casing from Italian sausage. Place crumbled sausage in a 9-inch glass pie plate with chopped mushroom stems and garlic. Microwave on high for 6 to 8 minutes, until sausage is cooked. Drain fat from sausage. Mix sausage mixture with dry bread crumbs, Romano cheese, fresh tarragon and fresh basil. Generously stuff mushroom caps with this mixture. Microwave mushroom caps on high until they are hot and steaming, 5 to 6 minutes. Serve immediately.

Serves: 8

MEXICAN PIZZA

Ingredients:
1 small onion, chopped
2 jalapeno peppers, seeded and chopped
2 ripe tomatoes
1/4 cup fresh cilantro, or parsley
1/2 teaspoon salt
4 corn or flour tortillas
1 cup Monterey Jack cheese, shredded
1 cup Cheddar cheese, shredded

Directions:
In blender cup, place onion, jalapenos, tomatoes, cilantro and salt. Blend until smooth, about 1 minute. Layer tortillas between paper towels and microwave on high for 1 minute to soften. In a 12-inch microwave dish or tray, place 2 tortillas. Top with tomato salsa and shredded cheeses. Top with second tortilla. Microwave on high for 3 minutes, until cheeses melt. Cut this double-faced Mexican pizza into 4 wedges and serve immediately.

Serves: 4

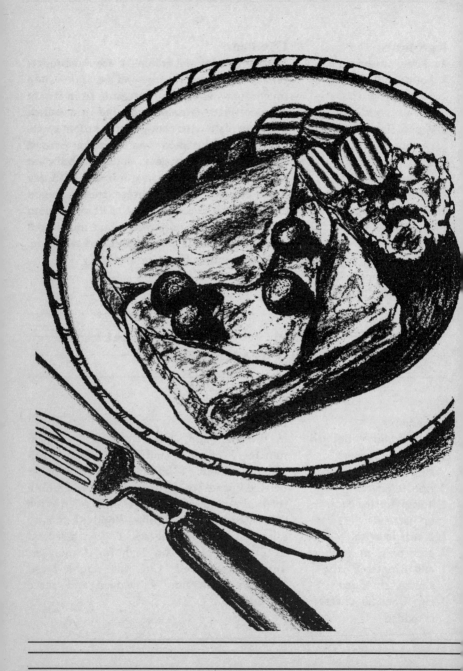

SHRIMP TOAST

Ingredients:
8 slices bread
1/4 cup butter
4 ounces Brie cheese (remove rind)
4 ounces Swiss cheese, shredded
1 egg, separated
6 ounces cooked salad shrimp
Black olive slices for garnish

Directions:
Toast bread and cut each slice into 4 triangles. Place toast on a microwave tray (you may need to do this in 2 batches). In a 2-cup microwave bowl, place butter and Brie cheese. Microwave for 30 seconds until butter melts and cheese is softened. Beat Swiss cheese and egg yolk into this mixture. In a separate bowl, beat egg white until soft peaks form. Fold this into the cheese mixture. Spread cheese mixture over toast triangles. Divide shrimp between triangles. Microwave on high until cheese melts, about 2 minutes for 16 triangles. Garnish with black olive slices.

Serves: Makes 32 shrimp toasts.

TINY AND TENDER BUTTER SCALLOPS

Ingredients:
3 tablespoons butter
1/2 teaspoon dill weed
1 pound tiny, bay scallops
1 cup button mushrooms
1/2 cup dry sherry
1/4 cup heavy cream

Directions:
Place butter in a microwave dish. Heat for 30 seconds to melt butter. Stir in dill weed, the scallops, mushrooms, and dry sherry. Cover and microwave on high for 4 to 6 minutes until the scallops are just firm. Add heavy cream, stir, cover, and heat on medium for 1 more minute. Serve immediately.

Serves: 4

RUMAKI

Ingredients:
1/2 pound sliced bacon
1 can whole water chestnuts
1/4 pound chicken livers, washed and patted dry
1/4 cup grape jelly
1/4 cup hot Chinese mustard

Directions:
Cut bacon slices in half. Wrap half of the slices of bacon around water chestnuts, skewering bacon and chestnut with a toothpick. Wrap remaining slices of bacon around chicken livers, skewering bacon into place with a toothpick. Line microwave proof bacon pan with paper toweling. Place bacon-chicken liver rumaki on pan. Microwave on high for 2 to 3 minutes. With bacon-chicken liver rumaki still on tray, add bacon-water chestnut rumaki and microwave on high until bacon is crisp and meat is cooked. Meanwhile, blend grape jelly with hot mustard. Serve on a decorative tray with a small bowl of mustard sauce for dipping.

Serves: 10

MICRO ROAST TENDERLOIN OF BEEF

Ingredients:
1 beef tenderloin, 2 to 2 1/2 pounds
1 envelope onion soup mix
1 pound fresh mushrooms, washed and sliced
1 large yellow onion, sliced

Directions:
Wet beef tenderloin; roll tenderloin in soup mix to coat well. Place in 9 x 13 glass dish. Cover roast with mushrooms and sliced onion. Cover glass dish loosely with plastic wrap. Microwave on high for 5 minutes. Turn dish and turn roast in dish. Cover and microwave on high for an additional 5 to 7 minutes or until it reaches desired doneness. Slice and serve hot or cold.

Serves: 4

MARINATED EYE OF ROUND ROAST

Ingredients:
1/4 cup vegetable oil
2 teaspoons lemon pepper seasoning
1/2 cup wine vinegar
1/2 cup lemon juice
1/2 cup soy sauce
1/2 cup Worcestershire sauce
1 (5 pound) eye of round roast

Directions:
Blend together oil, lemon pepper, vinegar, lemon juice, soy sauce, and Worcestershire. Pour over beef roast and allow to marinate for 2 to 3 days, turning once a day. Place beef with marinade in a 9 x 13 inch glass dish. Cover and microwave on high for 5 minutes. Turn dish. Microwave on low for 60 minutes, turning every 15 minutes. Refrigerate overnight. Slice thin and serve with marinade, heated. This will serve a crowd and makes great sandwiches.

Serves: 15

STUFFED MUSHROOMS, GREEK STYLE

Ingredients:

1 (10 ounce) package frozen chopped spinach

24 large mushrooms

1 tablespoon olive oil

1/2 cup green onions, chopped with tops

2 cloves garlic, minced

1/2 cup freshly grated Parmesan cheese

1/2 cup Feta cheese

1/2 cup fresh mint, chopped (or 2 tablespoons dried mint)

1 teaspoon salt

Mint leaves for garnish

Directions:

Place unopened package of spinach on a microwave plate. (Remove any foil wrapping from package before placing in microwave oven.) Microwave on high for 5 minutes. Remove spinach from package and drain thoroughly. Squeeze dry. Clean and stem mushrooms. Place mushroom caps on a large microwave tray and set aside. Chop mushroom stems and place in a 4-cup glass bowl with olive oil, onions, and garlic. Microwave on high for 4 to 5 minutes, until vegetables are tender. Blend spinach with vegetables, Parmesan cheese, Feta cheese, fresh or dried mint and salt. Fill mushroom caps with spinach mixture, mounding high in center. Microwave on high until mushrooms are very hot and steaming, about 5 to 6 minutes. Garnish with mint leaves and serve immediately.

Serves: 8

CELERY CASSEROLE WITH THREE CHEESES

Ingredients:
4 cups thinly sliced celery
1/2 cup butter
2 cups fresh mushrooms, sliced
2 tablespoons chopped green pepper
2 tablespoons chopped pimiento
1/4 cup flour
1 cup milk
1 cup grated Monterey Jack cheese with peppers
1/2 cup grated Cheddar cheese
1/2 cup freshly grated Parmesan cheese

Directions:
In a 2-quart microwave casserole, place celery and butter. Cover and microwave on high for 7 minutes until celery is just tender. Add mushrooms, green pepper, and pimiento; cover and microwave on high for 4 minutes. Stir together flour and milk. With a whisk, add flour and milk to vegetable mixture. Cover and microwave on medium for 2 minutes. Mixture will be smooth and hot. Top mixture with cheeses. Cover casserole, and microwave for 3 minutes at low heat. Cheese should be melted and casserole smooth and creamy. Serve immediately.

Serves: 6

POTATO SLICES WITH CHEESE

Ingredients:
4 potatoes, scrubbed
1 cup sour cream
1 cup farmer's cheese (if hard variety, grate)
2 cloves garlic, minced
1 small onion, chopped
1 teaspoon white pepper
Parsley for garnish
Paprika for garnish

Directions:
Slice potatoes with skins on. Place in a 1 quart microwave casserole. Add 1/2 cup water, cover tightly, and microwave on high for 10 minutes. Potatoes should be tender. Drain. Mix hot potatoes with sour cream, farmer's cheese, garlic, onion, and white pepper in the microwave casserole. Cover and microwave on medium for 8 minutes until bubbling and cheese is melted. Sprinkle with parsley and paprika. Serve immediately.

Serves: 6

CLASSIC CHICKEN WITH PARSLEY-CARAWAY DUMPLINGS

Ingredients:

1 frying chicken, cut up, about 3 pounds
2 bay leaves
1 cup celery, chopped
1 large onion, chopped
4 peppercorns
1 (15 ounce) can chicken broth
4 carrots, cut into slices
2 cups water
1/4 cup flour
1/2 cup water
Dumplings:
1 1/2 cups flour
2 teaspoons baking powder
1/4 cup chopped fresh parsley
2 teaspoons caraway seed
2/3 cup milk
1 egg

Directions:

In a large 4-quart microwave bowl, combine chicken with bay leaves, celery, onion, peppercorns, chicken broth, carrots, and 2 cups water. Cover and microwave on high for 25 minutes. Mix flour with 1/2 cup water and add to hot chicken mixture. Cover and microwave on medium for 2 minutes; stir to blend flour mixture with broth. Cover and microwave on medium an additional 6 minutes. If desired, remove chicken from microwave oven to strip meat from bones, then return meat to microwave bowl. *To make dumplings:* Blend flour, baking powder, parsley and caraway seed. Mix together milk and egg. Gently blend wet ingredients with dry ingredients. Drop spoons of dumpling mixture on top of stewed chicken in the microwave bowl. Cover bowl and microwave on high an additional 6 minutes. Dumplings will be firm. Serve immediately.

Serves: 6

CREAMY CHICKEN PAPRIKASH

Ingredients:

2 whole, boneless, skinless chicken breasts

2 tablespoons Hungarian or regular paprika

1/4 teaspoon cayenne pepper

1 large, yellow onion, chopped

2 cloves garlic, minced

1 green pepper, seeded and chopped

1/2 cup chicken stock (fresh or canned)

1 teaspoon salt

1/2 teaspoon freshly ground pepper

1 cup sour cream

2 cups hot, cooked noodles

Directions:

Rinse chicken breasts, split into 4 pieces and pat dry. Blend paprika and cayenne and work into chicken breasts. Place chicken with onion, garlic, green pepper, and chicken stock in a 3-quart microwave casserole. Cover and cook on high for 10 minutes; stir and turn; cover and cook on high an additional 6 minutes until chicken breasts are tender. Sprinkle with salt and pepper and mix sour cream throughout. Cover and microwave on medium for 2 more minutes. Serve with hot noodles.

Serves: 4

ASPARAGUS WITH TOASTED SESAME SEEDS

Ingredients:

1 pound fresh asparagus

1 cup fresh mushrooms, sliced

1 teaspoon lemon juice

2 tablespoons butter

1 teaspoon sesame seed, toasted

Directions:

Clean asparagus. Cut off any tough stems. Lay asparagus in glass dish. Top with mushrooms, lemon juice, and butter. Cover and microwave for 5 to 6 minutes until asparagus is just tender. Remove asparagus to a serving bowl. Top with sesame seed.

Serves: 4

BONELESS CHICKEN BREAST MARENGO

Ingredients:

3 whole boneless and skinless chicken breasts, about 2 pounds
2 tomatoes, chopped
1 cup celery, sliced
2 cups mushrooms, sliced
1 onion, chopped
3 cloves garlic, minced
1 cup chicken stock, (fresh or canned)
1 cup dry white wine
2 teaspoons arrowroot
1/4 cup water

Directions:

Cut chicken into 6 serving pieces. Place chicken in a 4-quart microwave casserole with tomatoes, celery, mushrooms, onion, garlic cloves, chicken stock and white wine. Cover and microwave on high for 20 minutes, turning the casserole and stirring once. Chicken should be tender and vegetables cooked. Blend arrowroot with 1/4 cup water and stir into hot chicken. Cover and microwave on medium for 2 minutes; stir, cover and microwave on medium an additional 6 minutes. Serve immediately.

Serves: 6

VEGETABLE STUFFED WALLEYE

Ingredients:

1 (1 1/2 pound) walleye pike, or 2 (12 ounce) trout
1/2 teaspoon salt
2 tablespoons butter
2 tablespoons chopped green onion
1 cup mushrooms, chopped
1 cup zucchini, grated
1 cup bread crumbs
1 egg
1 teaspoon fennel
1/3 cup white wine

Directions:

Wash fish, removing head and interior bones. Salt inside of fish. In a 2-quart microwave dish, place butter, green onion, mushrooms and zucchini. Cover and microwave on high for 5 minutes or until vegetables are tender. Add bread crumbs, egg, fennel, and white wine. Mix thoroughly. Stuff fish or fishes and secure with toothpicks. Place on microwave tray. Cover fish, and microwave on high for 8 minutes or until the thickest part is translucent and flesh flakes easily. Allow to stand for 2 minutes for easy carving. To serve: Remove stuffing from fish, and carve into 4 serving portions. Place on serving platter, and serve immediately.

Serves: 4

CALIFORNIA SLIM

Ingredients:
- 2 bunches broccoli
- 1 head cauliflower
- 2 tablespoons butter
- 1 small onion, chopped
- 1 clove garlic, minced
- 1 jalapeno pepper, minced
- 1/4 cup sunflower seeds

Directions:
Wash broccoli and separate flowerets from stems. Peel and chop broccoli stems. Wash cauliflower and separate flowerets from stems. Chop cauliflower stems. Mix broccoli and cauliflower flowerets and place around the edges of a round-bottom, 2-quart microwave bowl. Place stems in the middle of the bowl. *Slim sauce:* in a small microwave bowl, mix butter with onion, garlic, jalapeno, and sunflower seeds. Cover and microwave on high for 4 minutes until vegetables are tender and well blended. *For the cauliflower-broccoli presentation:* cover cauliflower-broccoli bowl and microwave on high for 12 minutes. Vegetables should be tender and steaming. Pack vegetables into bowl with the back of a wooden spoon, cover and microwave for 1 more minute. Remove cover, and invert microwave dish onto a serving plate. Remove dish to reveal a perfectly rounded mound of cauliflower-broccoli. Pour hot sauce over the vegetables and serve immediately.

Serves: 8

FRESH SEAFOOD FILLETS WITH VEGETABLES

Ingredients:

1 cup zucchini slices

1 medium-sized red pepper, sliced

1 cup snow peas, washed and stemmed

1 medium sized onion, sliced

1 cup sliced celery

1 cup broccoli flowerets

4 to 6 ounces fresh fish fillets (flounder, snapper, perch, sole)

1 teaspoon fresh basil, chopped (or 1/2 teaspoon dried basil)

1/2 teaspoon dried chervil

1 teaspoon salt

1 tablespoon olive oil

2 teaspoons freshly squeezed lemon juice

Paprika for garnish

Directions:

Combine zucchini with red pepper, snow peas, onion, celery and broccoli in a microwave casserole. Sprinkle with 2 tablespoons water. Cover and microwave on high for 8 minutes until vegetables are tender-crisp. Remove casserole from microwave but allow to remain covered to retain heat. In a second microwave dish, place fish fillets. Sprinkle with fresh basil, chervil, salt, and olive oil. Cover and microwave on high for 6 to 8 minutes. Fillets are cooked when the meat is translucent and the flesh flakes easily. To serve: place fish in the center of a platter. Arrange vegetables around the edges. Top with lemon juice and paprika.

Serves: 4

GERMAN BURGERS

Ingredients:

1/2 cup crushed gingersnaps

1 (10 3/4 ounce) can cream of mushroom soup

1 small onion, chopped

1 pound lean ground beef

2 tablespoons brown sugar

2 tablespoons vinegar

1 teaspoon prepared mustard

1 teaspoon black pepper

1/3 cup water

4 kaiser rolls

Directions:

Mix gingersnaps with 2 tablespoons of the mushroom soup, and the onion. Add ground beef and mix well. Form into 4 large beef patties and place in a glass casserole, 8 x 8 x 2 inches. Cover and microwave on high for 3 minutes. Turn casserole and microwave on high for 2 more minutes. Meanwhile, combine remaining mushroom soup with brown sugar, vinegar, mustard, pepper, and 1/3 cup water. Pour over meat. Cover and microwave on high for 3 minutes longer. Serve on toasted kaiser rolls.

Serves: 4

TEX MEX STUFFED TOMATOES

Ingredients:

6 large, ripe tomatoes

2 tablespoons butter

1 jalapeno pepper, minced

1 clove garlic, minced

1/2 cup green onions, chopped

1 medium green pepper, chopped

1/2 cup chopped cilantro (or use fresh parsley)

1/4 crushed corn chips

1/2 cup Monterey Jack cheese

Cilantro sprigs for garnish

Corn chips for garnish

Directions:

Cut off tops of tomatoes and hollow out inside. Place hollowed-out tomatoes on microwave tray. Coarsely chop tomato interior and place in a medium-sized microwave bowl with butter, jalapeno, garlic, onions, green pepper, and cilantro. Cover bowl and microwave on high for 4 minutes or until vegetables are tender. Blend in corn chips and cheese and stuff tomatoes lightly with mixture. Microwave, uncovered, on high for 5 minutes, or until heated through and cheese is melted. Garnish with cilantro sprig and extra corn chips.

Serves: 6

FRESH SALMON RING

Ingredients:

1 pound fresh salmon
3 eggs, beaten
1 cup seasoned bread
  crumbs
1 cup celery, finely
  chopped
1 medium green pepper,
  chopped
1 small yellow onion,
  chopped
3/4 cup half-and-half
1 tablespoon lemon
  juice
1/4 cup fresh chopped
  parsley
1 hard-cooked egg for
  garnish
Parsley sprigs for
  garnish

Directions:

In a 9-inch, glass pie plate, place salmon. Cover and microwave on high for 5 to 7 minutes. Salmon should be cooked and translucent and flesh should flake easily. Cool. Blend flaked salmon with eggs, bread crumbs, celery, green pepper, onion, half-and-half, lemon juice and chopped parsley. Blend well. Pack mixture into a 3-quart microwave ring mold. Cover and microwave on high for 8 minutes. Fresh salmon loaf will be pulled away from sides and firmly set. Allow to rest for 5 minutes; then, unmold on round serving platter and garnish with hard-cooked egg slices and parsley sprigs.

Serves: 6

GREEN PEPPERS WITH CHICKEN AND CORN STUFFING

Ingredients:
4 large green peppers
1 large, ripe tomato, chopped
1 medium-sized onion, chopped
2 cloves garlic, minced
1 pound ground chicken (or ground turkey)
1 cup fresh or frozen corn kernels
1/4 cup chopped parsley
1 cup fine dry bread crumbs
1 egg
1/2 cup grated Cheddar cheese

Directions:
Stem, core, and seed green peppers. Place in a 9-inch, glass pie plate, cover and microwave on high for 2 minutes, until peppers are just starting to become tender. Place tomato, onion, garlic, and ground chicken in a 1 1/2-quart microwave dish; cover and microwave on high for 10 minutes, stirring and turning one time. Chicken should be cooked and vegetables tender. Blend in corn, parsley, breadcrumbs, and egg. Mix thoroughly. Stuff green peppers with chicken mixture. Cover and microwave on high for 4 minutes. Top with Cheddar cheese, cover and microwave for an additional 3 minutes.

Serves: 4

GREEN BEANS, CAESAR STYLE

Ingredients:
1 pound fresh green beans, tips removed and cut into 1-inch lengths
1 small onion, minced
2 tablespoons wine vinegar
2 tablespoons olive oil
1 cup herb croutons
1/4 cup freshly grated Parmesan cheese
4 anchovy fillets, chopped (optional)

Directions:
In a 1-quart microwave casserole, combine green beans with onion, vinegar, and olive oil. Cover and microwave on high for 6 to 8 minutes, or until beans are tender. Stir in croutons and sprinkle with Parmesan cheese and chopped anchovy fillets.

Serves: 4

CONNIE'S MASHED POTATOES ... THE CHILDREN'S FAVORITE

Ingredients:
1 (3 ounce) package cream cheese
1/2 cup sour cream
1 teaspoon onion salt
1 teaspoon white pepper
1 egg
1/2 cup white Cheddar, shredded
3 cups mashed potatoes (instant, home cooked, or leftover)

Directions:
In a 2-quart microwave casserole, place cream cheese. Cover and microwave on high for 1 minute until cream cheese is very soft. Blend in sour cream, onion salt, pepper, egg, and Cheddar cheese. Blend in potatoes, a little at a time, until well blended. Cover casserole and microwave on high for 10 to 12 minutes. Cheese should be melted and potatoes bubbly.

Serves: 6

OLD FASHIONED BEEF LOAF WITH CHILLI SAUCE

Ingredients:
1 1/2 pounds lean ground beef
1 medium sized yellow onion, chopped
2 cloves garlic, minced
1 teaspoon Worcestershire sauce
1 cup oatmeal
2 eggs
1/2 cup milk
1/2 teaspoon mustard
1/2 teaspoon freshly grated black pepper
1/2 cup chilli sauce
Parsley sprigs for garnish

Directions:
Blend ground beef with onion, garlic, Worcestershire sauce, oatmeal, eggs, milk, mustard, and black pepper. Pack into a microwave ring mold. Cover and microwave on high for 10 minutes or until beef loaf starts to pull from sides of mold. Allow to rest for 5 minutes. Invert onto serving platter, top with chilli sauce, and garnish with parsley sprigs.

Serves: 4

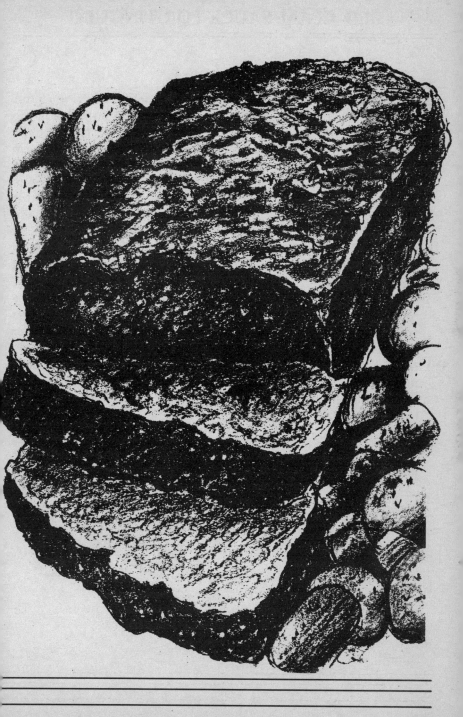

RED CLAM SAUCE FOR LINGUINE

Ingredients:
3 quarts water
1 cup cornmeal
3 to 4 dozen clams
2 large, ripe tomatoes, chopped
1/2 cup chopped onion
4 cloves garlic, minced
1 tablespoon olive oil
1/4 cup chopped, fresh parsley
1/2 teaspoon dried oregano
1/4 cup chopped, fresh basil (or 2 tablespoons dried basil)
1 cup dry red wine, (Italian)
2 tablespoons chopped, fresh parsley for garnish
1 pound cooked linguine

Directions:
Soak clams in a solution of 3 quarts water to 1 cup of cornmeal; then, scrub shells carefully to remove any sand or dirt. In a large, 4-quart microwave casserole, place clams with 1/2 cup water. Cover and microwave on high for 6 to 8 minutes until all clams open. (As clams open, remove them from casserole. This allows other clams more cooking time). Remove clams from shells, reserve clams and discard shells. Drain liquid from large casserole into a 2-quart microwave dish. To this dish, add tomatoes, onion, garlic, olive oil, parsley, oregano and basil. Cover and microwave for 6 to 8 minutes, until tomatoes are soft and vegetables are tender. Pour into blender cup or food processor and process until very smooth. Return puree to casserole along with cooked clams and red wine. Microwave, covered, on high for 3 minutes, just to heat sauce. Serve over cooked linguine.

Serves: 4

SEAFOOD VERACRUZ

Ingredients:

2 large, ripe tomatoes, chopped

1 large green pepper, seeded and cut into chunks

1 large yellow onion, sliced

2 cloves garlic, minced

2 tablespoons olive oil

1/4 cup dry white wine

1/4 cup fresh chopped parsley

1 teaspoon chervil

1/2 teaspoon dried oregano

1 teaspoon cumin

1 teaspoon cayenne pepper

1/2 pound uncooked shrimp, shelled, de-veined, and cleaned

1/2 pound ocean scallops, cut into halves

1/2 pound fresh whitefish, cut into 1-inch pieces

2 tablespoons fresh, chopped parsley for garnish

2 cups hot, cooked rice

Directions:

Combine tomatoes, green pepper, onion, garlic, olive oil, white wine, parsley, chervil, oregano, cumin, and cayenne pepper in a 3-quart microwave casserole. Cover and microwave for 10 minutes, until vegetables are tender-crisp. Add shrimp, scallops and whitefish, and stir to coat with vegetables and sauce. Cover and microwave for 8 to 10 minutes, until shrimp turn pink and firm to touch and fish flakes easily. Serve in shallow bowls with chopped parsley over hot, cooked rice.

Serves: 4

TERIYAKI MEATBALLS WITH ORIENTAL SAUCE

Ingredients:
1 pound ground beef
1 egg
1 medium onion,
  chopped
1/2 cup drained water
  chestnuts, chopped
2 tablespoons fine dry
  bread crumbs
1 teaspoon teriyaki
  sauce
1/8 teaspoon pepper
1 (15 ounce) can
  pineapple chunks
  (reserve 1/2 cup
  juice)
1/2 cup water
2 tablespoons vinegar
2 tablespoons cornstarch
1 tablespoon brown
  sugar, packed
2 tablespoons soy sauce
2 cups hot, cooked rice
  or fried rice

Directions:
Blend together ground beef, egg, onion, water chestnuts, bread crumbs, teriyaki sauce and pepper. Form into 24 meatballs. Place in a 2-quart microwave casserole. Cover and microwave on high for 3 minutes. Rotate dish and microwave 3 more minutes. Drain fat from casserole. Blend pineapple chunks, pineapple juice, 1/2 cup water, vinegar, cornstarch, brown sugar and soy sauce. Pour over meatballs, turning meatballs so that they are completely covered by sauce. Cover and microwave on high for 2 more minutes; turn dish, stir, and microwave for 2 more minutes. Serve over hot, cooked rice or fried rice.

Serves: 4

HOMESTYLE TUNA WITH NOODLES

Ingredients:

1 (8 ounce) package frozen noodles
1 cup chopped celery
1/4 cup chopped onion
2 tablespoons butter
2 tablespoons flour
1 cup shredded Cheddar cheese
1 cup half-and-half
1 (7 ounce) can tuna, packed in water
1/4 cup chopped pimiento
1/2 cup fresh chopped parsley
1/4 cup grated Parmesan cheese

Directions:

Remove any foil wrapping from package of noodles and place noodles in microwave. Using defrost cycle, defrost for 2 to 3 minutes. Remove noodles from package. In a 1 1/2-quart microwave casserole, place celery, onion and butter. Cover and microwave on high for 4 minutes or until vegetables are tender. Whisk in flour; cover and microwave for 2 minutes on medium. Whisk in Cheddar cheese and half-and-half, cover, and microwave for 5 minutes. The sauce will be thick and smooth. Drain tuna; and carefully stir tuna, noodles, pimiento and parsley into casserole. Cover and microwave for 4 to 5 minutes. Mixture will be heated through and creamy. Sprinkle Parmesan cheese over top of casserole.

Serves: 6

HOT 'N' SPICY GLAZED CARROTS

Ingredients:

6 large carrots, julienne
2 tablespoons butter
2 tablespoons honey
1 teaspoon cayenne pepper
1/2 teaspoon cinnamon
1/4 teaspoon hot sauce
1/2 teaspoon salt

Directions:

Julienne carrots by peeling, then cutting into very thin strips. Place carrots with butter, honey, cayenne, cinnamon, hot sauce and salt into a 1 1/2-quart microwave casserole. Cover and microwave on high for 8 to 10 minutes. Carrots will be tender, and sauce, thickened. Serve immediately.

Serves: 6

VERY QUICK AND EASY LASAGNA

Ingredients:
1 cup ricotta cheese
1 egg
1/4 cup chopped parsley
8 ounces lasagna noodles (regular or whole wheat)
2 cups canned tomato meat sauce
4 ounces sliced mozzarella cheese
4 ounces grated Provolone cheese
4 ounces freshly grated Parmesan cheese

Directions:
Blend together ricotta cheese, egg and parsley. In bottom of 8 x 8 x 2 inch glass casserole, place a layer of UNCOOKED lasagna noodles. Top with 1/4 cup ricotta cheese, 1/2 cup meat sauce, and sliced mozzarella cheese. Next layer more uncooked lasagna noodles, ricotta cheese, meat sauce, Provolone and Parmesan cheese. Repeat for 2 more layers ending with a covering of sauce. Cover dish very tightly with plastic wrap and place in microwave oven. Microwave on low for 15 minutes; turn dish and microwave on low for 15 minutes; turn dish and microwave on low for 15 more minutes. If lasagna noodles are not fork tender microwave on low for a few more minutes. Allow to rest for 10 minutes before cutting.

Serves: 4

HOT MAPLE TODDY WITH WHISKEY

Ingredients:
1 cup whiskey
1 cup maple syrup
3/4 cup orange juice
2 cups freshly brewed coffee
1 teaspoon vanilla extract
2 teaspoons sugar
4 pats butter
4 cinnamon sticks

Directions:
In a 2-quart glass measuring cup, combine whiskey, maple syrup, orange juice, coffee, vanilla and sugar. Microwave on high for 6 to 8 minutes, until heated through and sugar is melted. Pour into 4 heated mugs. Top each with a pat of butter and add cinnamon sticks.

Serves: 4

MASHED SWEETS WITH CARMEL TOPPING

Ingredients:

4 large sweet potatoes, cooked, peeled and puréed (or mashed)

2 tablespoons butter

3 tablespoons orange juice

1/4 teaspoon allspice

1/2 teaspoon black pepper

1/4 cup fresh chopped parsley

3 tablespoons pecans, chopped

1/3 cup brown sugar, firmly packed

Directions:

In a 2-quart microwave casserole, combine sweet potatoes with butter, orange juice, allspice, black pepper, and parsley. Mix well. Sprinkle with pecans and brown sugar. Cover and microwave on high for 6 minutes or until hot.

Serves: 6

MIXED PEPPER QUICHE

Ingredients:

1 medium green pepper, chopped

1 medium red pepper, chopped

2 small jalapeno peppers, chopped

2 medium-sized mild banana peppers, chopped

1 medium yellow onion, chopped

1 clove garlic, minced

2 tablespoons olive oil

3/4 cup half-and-half

3 large eggs

2 tablespoons chopped cilantro (or parsley)

Directions:

Place all peppers with onion, garlic and olive oil in a 9-inch, glass pie plate. Cover and microwave on high for 6 minutes until vegetables are tender. Beat together the half-and-half and eggs. Carefully pour egg mixture over the vegetables. Cover and microwave on medium for 15 minutes, turning the pie plate every 3 to 4 minutes. Sprinkle quiche with cilantro and allow to rest for 5 minutes before cutting.

Serves: 6

BAKED STUFFED POTATOES

Ingredients:

4 large Idaho baking potatoes, well scrubbed

4 thin slices prosciutto ham

4 ounces Brie cheese

4 medium-sized eggs

1/4 cup freshly grated Parmesan cheese

Chopped parsley for garnish

Paprika for garnish

Directions:

Prick potatoes and microwave on high for a total of 16 to 18 minutes. Allow to cool. Make a potato shell by removing a section of the top of the potato and 1/2 cup of interior of potato. Place potato shells on a microwave tray. Into potato shell, put a slice of prosciutto ham. Top that with several slices of Brie cheese. Carefully break an egg into the potato shell on top of ham and cheese. Sprinkle egg with grated Parmesan cheese and microwave all four potatoes (together) on high for 8 minutes until the egg is set and cheese starts to melt. Garnish potato tops with chopped parsley and paprika.

Serves: 4

MOM'S CHEESEY CAULIFLOWER

Ingredients:

1 head fresh cauliflower

1/2 cup mayonnaise

1 small yellow onion, chopped

1 teaspoon Dijon mustard

1/2 cup sharp Cheddar, grated

Directions:

Clean cauliflower and separate flowerets. Place flowerets in 2-quart microwave dish. Cover and microwave on high for 6 minutes or until cauliflower is tender. Mix together mayonnaise, onion, mustard and cheese. Pour over cauliflower flowerets. Cover and microwave on medium for 2 minutes or until cheese melts and sauce is well blended with cauliflower.

Serves: 4

PEARLS AND PEAS WITH CREMINI MUSHROOMS

Ingredients:
1 cup pearl onions
1 cup water
2 tablespoons olive oil
1 clove garlic, minced
1 cup cremini (or button) mushrooms, washed and sliced very thin
1 (10 ounce) package frozen tiny peas
1/4 cup chopped mint
1/2 teaspoon white pepper
1/8 teaspoon allspice

Directions:
In a medium-sized microwave bowl, place pearl onions and 1 cup water. Cover and microwave on high for 3 minutes. Drain pearl onions, cool, then cut stem end of onion and slip onion out of its tough skin. In medium-sized microwave bowl, place olive oil, garlic, mushrooms, and frozen peas. Cover and microwave on high for 6 minutes. Peas should be defrosted and mushrooms, tender. Add onions to mushroom mixture and add mint, pepper and allspice. Cover and microwave on high for 3 minutes, to heat and blend flavors.

Serves: 4

BROCCOLI TOMATO MELT, SWISS STYLE

Ingredients:
2 large, ripe tomatoes, sliced into 1/2-inch slices
2 bunches broccoli
2 tablespoons butter
2 tablespoons flour
1 cup half-and-half
1 cup Swiss cheese, grated

Directions:
Arrange sliced tomatoes on a round serving platter. Rinse broccoli. Cut off flowerets. Peel stems and slice into 1-inch slices. Place stems in a 2-quart microwave dish, cover, and microwave on high for 4 minutes. Add flowerets, and microwave for an additional 4 minutes. Broccoli should be tender-crisp. Drain. In small microwave dish, blend butter, flour and half-and-half. Cover and microwave for 1 minute. Whisk sauce to smooth, and add cheese. Cover and microwave on medium for 3 minutes or until cheese melts. Arrange broccoli atop tomato slices, and pour Swiss cheese over all. Serve immediately.

Serves: 6

RED CABBAGE, PENNSYLVANIA STYLE

Ingredients:
2 tablespoons olive oil
1/4 cup brown sugar, packed
1/4 cup vinegar
1 teaspoon caraway seed
1 teaspoon cayenne pepper
1 teaspoon paprika
4 cups shredded red cabbage
2 large Rome apples, peeled, cored, seeded and cubed

Directions:
In a 3-quart microwave casserole, combine olive oil, brown sugar, vinegar, caraway seed, cayenne pepper and paprika. Cover and microwave on high for 2 minutes. Add cabbage and apples. Cover and microwave on high for 10 minutes or until cabbage is very tender and blended with other ingredients.

Serves: 6

SPINACH AND ARTICHOKE DELIGHT

Ingredients:
2 pounds spinach, washed, rewashed, and stemmed
1/4 cup butter
4 tablespoons flour
1 cup milk
1 medium onion, chopped
4 cloves garlic, minced
1/2 cup jalapeno cheese
1 (14 ounce) can artichoke hearts
1 cup rice, cooked
1 cup herb stuffing
1 (8 ounce) can sliced mushrooms

Directions:
Place spinach in a very large, microwave casserole. Cover and microwave on high for 15 minutes. Drain spinach, reserving 1/2 cup liquid. In a 1-quart microwave bowl, blend butter with flour, spinach liquid, milk, onion and garlic. Cover and microwave on high for 2 minutes. Whisk to blend ingredients; microwave on medium for 2 minutes. Whisk to take out any lumps. Add cheese to sauce. Drain and quarter artichokes and add to sauce. Add rice, stuffing and mushrooms which have been drained. Add sauce to the spinach that is in the large, microwave casserole, cover and microwave on high for 2 minutes. Mixture will be steaming. Serve immediately.

Serves: 6

BRUSSELS SPROUTS WITH YELLOW SAUCE

Ingredients:
1 pound fresh Brussels sprouts
2 tablespoons butter
1 small onion, chopped
2 cloves garlic, minced
2 tablespoons flour
1 cup half-and-half
1 tablespoon chopped chives
2 teaspoons freshly squeezed lemon juice

Directions:
Wash and clean Brussels sprouts. Remove outer leaves and make a small X with a knife in the stem end of the Brussels sprout. This will enable sprouts to cook more evenly. Place Brussels sprouts in a 2-quart microwave casserole. In a 1-quart microwave casserole, blend butter with onion and garlic. Cover and microwave on high for 3 minutes. Vegetables should be tender. Whisk in flour and half-and-half. Cover and microwave on medium for 2 minutes. Whisk again, and add chives and lemon juice. Cover and microwave on medium for 2 minutes. Whisk sauce to remove any lumps. Cover Brussels sprouts casserole and microwave on high for 10 minutes. Brussels sprouts should be evenly tender. Drain off any liquid and pour butter-lemon sauce over hot vegetable. Serve immediately.

Serves: 6

CINNAMON SQUASH BAKE

Ingredients:

- 1 medium sized butternut (or acorn) squash, (1 pound)
- 1 tablespoon butter
- 1 tablespoon lemon juice
- 2 Jonathan apples, cored and chopped
- 1/4 cup orange juice
- 1/4 teaspoon cinnamon
- 1/4 teaspoon ground cloves
- 1 tablespoon honey
- 1 tablespoon chopped pecans

Directions:

Scrub squash to remove surface dirt. Prick skin and microwave on high for 10 minutes. Allow to cool slightly, cut in half and remove seeds. Cover the two halves of squash and continue to cook on high for 5 to 10 minutes, until the squash is tender. Remove squash from skin and purée. Pour squash purée into a microwave bowl, and set aside. In a 1-quart microwave bowl, blend butter with lemon juice, apples, orange juice, cinnamon, cloves and honey. Cover and microwave on high for 3 to 4 minutes, until the apples are tender. Purée this mixture. Fold apple mixture into the squash mixture, cover and microwave on high for 2 minutes. Sprinkle with pecans and serve piping hot.

Serves: 4

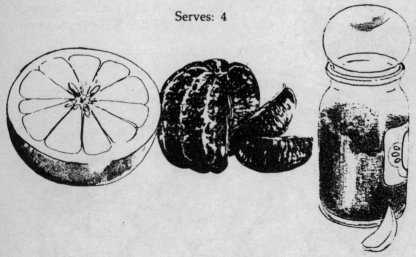

CONTINENTAL SQUASH

Ingredients:

10 to 12 small yellow
   squash (or patty pan
   or zucchini)
1 1/2 pounds bacon
8 green onions with
   tops, chopped
1 1/2 large yellow
   onions, chopped
2 tablespoons fresh
   chopped parsley
1 medium green pepper,
   chopped
1 cup freshly grated
   Parmesan cheese
1 cup seasoned, dry
   bread crumbs
Chopped chives for
   garnish
Paprika for garnish

Directions:

Wash and slice squash. Place in a 4-quart microwave casserole. Cover and microwave on high for 14 to 16 minutes, until squash are tender. Drain. On a microwave bacon tray, layer bacon. Microwave on high for 20 minutes. Cool and crumble bacon. In a 1-quart microwave bowl, place 1/4 cup bacon fat, green and yellow onions, parsley and green pepper. Cover and microwave for 5 minutes until vegetables are tender. Blend cooked squash with crumbled bacon, cooked vegetables, Parmesan cheese and dry bread crumbs. Place in a microwave casserole, cover and microwave on medium for 5 to 7 minutes, until casserole is hot and bubbly. Sprinkle with chopped chives and paprika. Serve immediately.

Serves: 8

CHINESE FRIED RICE

Ingredients:
1 1/2 cups long grain
    or brown rice
3 cups water
3 tablespoons vegetable
    oil (preferably peanut
    oil)
1/2 cup smoked ham,
    finely chopped
1/4 cup mushrooms,
    finely chopped
1/4 cup green onions,
    thinly sliced
2 eggs, beaten
3 tablespoons soy sauce

Directions:
In a 2-quart microwave casserole, place rice with 3 cups cold water. Cover and microwave on high for 12 to 13 minutes, until water is absorbed and rice is tender. In a 3-quart microwave casserole, place vegetable oil, ham, mushrooms, and onions. Cover and microwave on high for 4 minutes. The ham will be cooked and the vegetables, tender. Blend hot rice into this mixture. Add eggs and soy sauce and mix very well. Cover and microwave on high for 3 to 4 minutes to set eggs and blend flavors.

Serves: 6

TEX MEX CHILLI

Ingredients:
- 2 pounds beef chuck roast
- 1 large onion, chopped
- 1 medium-sized green pepper, chopped
- 1 jalapeno pepper, minced
- 1 clove garlic, minced
- 2 tablespoons chilli powder
- 1 teaspoon cumin
- 1/4 cup fresh cilantro or parsley, chopped
- 3 large, ripe tomatoes, chopped
- 1 teaspoon dried oregano
- 1 cup beef stock

Directions:
Trim chuck roast, then cut into 1-inch chunks. Blend beef with remaining ingredients in a 3-quart microwave casserole. Stir well. Cover and microwave on high for 7 minutes. Turn casserole and stir. Microwave on medium for 30 to 40 minutes, turning casserole and stirring the chilli every 10 to 12 minutes. Serve with corn chips and chopped onion.

Serves: 6

ITALIAN STYLE GREEN BEANS WITH SAUSAGE AND CHEESE

Ingredients:
- 2 packages frozen Italian green beans
- 1/2 pound hot Italian sausage, casing removed
- 1 (8 ounce) can tomato sauce
- 2 tablespoon prepared mustard
- 1 small onion, chopped
- 2 cloves garlic, minced
- 1 tablespoon olive oil
- 1/2 cup Provolone cheese, grated

Directions:
Remove any foil wrapping from packages of beans and microwave beans, in packages, on high for 6 minutes until defrosted. Remove beans from packaging and place in a 2-quart microwave casserole. In a 1-quart microwave casserole, crumble sausage. Cover and microwave on high for 5 minutes, until sausage is cooked. Drain. Combine beans, sausage, tomato sauce, mustard, onion, garlic and olive oil in the 2-quart microwave casserole. Cover and microwave on high for 6 minutes or until beans are tender. Sprinkle cheese atop and microwave on high for 1 minute.

Serves: 6

BLUEBERRY DUMP CAKE

Ingredients:
1 (21 ounce) can
   blueberry pie filling
2 medium sized baking
   apples, Jonathan,
   Rome, or Granny
   Smith
Juice of 2 lemons (4
   tablespoons)
1/2 cup butter
1 (9 ounce) yellow cake
   mix
3/4 cup walnuts,
   chopped
1 cup sweetened
   whipped cream

Directions:
In a 2-quart microwave baking dish, 'dump'
blueberry pie filling. Spread evenly. Peel, core,
and dice apples. Sprinkle with lemon juice.
Spread apples over blueberry pie filling. Cut
butter into cake mix until crumbly. Sprinkle
this mixture over apples. Top with walnuts.
Cover and microwave on high for 8 to 10
minutes; serve warm with sweetened whipped
cream.

Serves: 8

CREAMY HOT MOCHA

Ingredients:
2 cups half-and-half
1/4 cup sugar
1/2 cup unsweetened
   cocoa
1 1/2 teaspoons vanilla
   extract
2 cups strong coffee
   (preferably
   Columbian)
2 cups water
8 cinnamon sticks
1 cup sweetened
   whipped cream

Directions:
In a 2-quart glass bowl, combine half-and-
half and sugar. Cover and microwave on high
for 5 minutes, until half-and-half is hot.
Whisk sugar to blend and whisk in
unsweetened cocoa. Add vanilla, coffee, and
water. Cover and microwave on high for an
additional 5 minutes, stirring after 3 minutes.
Pour into 8 mugs, add a cinnamon stick for
sipping, and top with sweetened whipped
cream.

Serves: 8

CRUNCHY GRANOLA SQUARES

Ingredients:
1/4 cup butter
1 1/2 cups granola cereal (homemade or packaged)
2 medium-sized baking apples, (Jonathan, Rome, or Granny Smith)
1 package butterscotch-flavored morsels
1 (14 ounce) can sweetened condensed milk (not evaporated milk)
1 cup flaked coconut
1 cup pecans, chopped

Directions:
In a 9 x 9 x 2 square glass microwave dish, place butter. Cover and microwave on high for 30 seconds. Sprinkle granola over butter and press to form crust on the bottom of dish. Peel, core and chop apples. Top granola with apples. In a 1-quart microwave dish, combine butterscotch morsels with milk. Cover and microwave on medium for 2 to 3 minutes, until morsels are melted. Pour butterscotch mixture over apple mixture. Top with coconut and pecans. Cover and microwave on high for 8 to 10 minutes, turning every 2 minutes. Chill before cutting into bars.

Serves: Makes 12 bars

DARK AND DELICIOUS CHOCOLATE PECAN PIE

Ingredients:
1/4 cup butter
1 cup brown sugar, packed
1/2 cup dark corn syrup
3 eggs, beaten
1 teaspoon vanilla
1 cup whole pecans
1 cup chocolate morsels or chunks
1 baked, 9-inch pie shell (in glass or other microwaveable pie plate)

Directions:
In a 2-quart dish, place butter with brown sugar, corn syrup, eggs, vanilla, and pecans. Mix well. Sprinkle chocolate morsels in the bottom of pie shell. Top with pecan mixture. Place in microwave oven and microwave on high for 8 to 10 minutes until top of pie is just set. Allow to cool for 2 hours before serving.

Serves: 8

PUMPKIN-BRAN MUFFINS

Ingredients:
1 cup buttermilk
2 teaspoons baking
  powder
1 cup pumpkin purée,
  (fresh or canned)
1 cup brown sugar,
  packed
1/2 teaspoon salt
3/4 cup vegetable oil
  (preferably safflower)
2 eggs
1 cup flour
2/3 cup wheat or oat
  bran
1 cup walnuts, chopped
2 teaspoons pumpkin
  pie spice

Directions:
In a medium-sized mixing bowl, blend buttermilk with baking powder, pumpkin, brown sugar, and salt. Allow the mixture to cure for 5 minutes. It will become bubbly. Mix together vegetable oil and eggs. Blend flour with bran, walnuts, and pumpkin pie spice. Blend buttermilk mixture with egg mixture, and pour wet ingredients into dry ingredients. Mix only until dry mixture is wet; do not overmix. Divide batter between 12 microwave proof muffin pans which have been lined with paper muffin liners. (If you do not have a microwave muffin pan you may use 1 cup glass custard cups; place 6 custard cups at a time in a circle on a round microwave safe platter.) Microwave on high for 4 1/2 minutes, turning muffin pans or platters every minute. Serve muffins warm.

Serves: 12

LEMON CHIFFON PIE IN CHOCOLATE CRUMB CRUST

Ingredients:

1 1/4 cups fine ground
chocolate wafer
crumbs
2 tablespoons sugar
1/4 cup butter, melted
1 envelope unflavored
gelatin
1 cup water
1/2 cup sugar
4 eggs, separated
1/4 cup freshly
squeezed lemon juice
1/4 cup sugar
Grated lemon peel from
1 lemon

Directions:

Blend chocolate wafer crumbs with sugar and butter. Press firmly onto the sides and bottom of a 9-inch, glass pie plate. Microwave on high for 2 minutes, rotating plate one-half turn after 1 minute. Cool. In a 1-quart microwave dish, combine unflavored gelatin with 1 cup water. Allow this mixture to soak until gelatin expands, about 5 minutes. Meanwhile beat egg yolks till thick and lemon colored. Add lemon juice and 1/2 cup sugar. Pour egg mixture into gelatin mixture. Cover and microwave on high for 2 minutes, stirring every 30 seconds. The mixture will almost come to a boil. Beat with an electric mixer until cooled and very smooth. In a very clean bowl, beat egg whites until foamy. Sprinkle 1/4 cup sugar, 1 tablespoon at a time, over egg whites. Continue to beat until soft peaks form. Fold egg yolk mixture into egg white mixture and, gently, into the prepared crust. Sprinkle with grated lemon peel. Chill for 4 hours before serving.

Serves: 8

PUMPKIN CHIFFON PIE IN GINGERSNAP CRUST

Ingredients:

1 1/4 cups finely ground gingersnaps

2 tablespoons sugar

1/4 cup butter, softened

1 envelope unflavored gelatin

1/2 cup brown sugar, packed

1/2 teaspoon cinnamon

2 cups pumpkin purée, (fresh or canned)

1/2 cup half-and-half

1/4 teaspoon vanilla extract

4 large eggs, separated

2 tablespoons sugar

1 cup sweetened whipped cream

Directions:

In a 9-inch, glass pie plate, combine gingersnaps, sugar, and butter. Press along sides and bottom of pie plate. Microwave on high for 2 minutes. Cool. In a 2-quart microwave bowl, soften gelatin by soaking it in 2 tablespoons water for 5 minutes. Add brown sugar, cinnamon, pumpkin, milk, and vanilla extract. Cover and microwave on high for 3 to 4 minutes. Beat egg yolks until thick and lemon colored. Add 1/2 cup of hot pumpkin to egg yolks to heat them, then stir the egg mixture into the pumpkin mixture. Beat egg whites until foamy; sprinkle with sugar, 1 tablespoon at a time, and beat until soft peaks form. Fold meringue into pumpkin mixture. Spoon into cooled pie shell. Chill for 4 hours or overnight. Serve with sweetened whipped cream.

Serves: 8

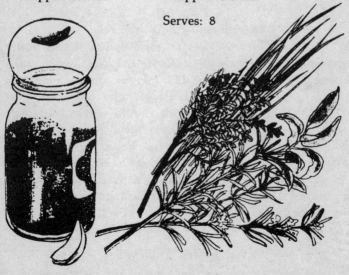

BUTTERSCOTCH FLAVORED POTATO CHIPS

Ingredients:
- 1 (14 ounce) can sweetened condensed milk, (not evaporated milk)
- 1 (6 ounce) package butterscotch-flavored morsels
- 1 cup crunchy style peanut butter
- 2 cups regular style potato chips
- 1 cup peanuts, chopped finely

Directions:
In a 2-quart microwave dish, combine milk, butterscotch morsels, and peanut butter. Cover and microwave on high for 4 minutes, stirring after 2 minutes. Carefully coat both sides of potato chips with butterscotch mixture. While still warm, sprinkle with peanuts. Allow to set for 10 minutes.

Serves: Makes 2 pounds

DOUBLE CHOCOLATE BROWNIES WITH PECANS

Ingredients:
- 1/2 cup butter
- 2 ounces unsweetened baking chocolate
- 2 eggs
- 1/2 cup sugar
- 2 teaspoons vanilla
- 1/2 cup flour
- 1 teaspoon baking powder
- 1 cup pecans, chopped
- 1 cup chocolate morsels

Directions:
In a 2-quart microwave dish, blend butter with chocolate. Cover and microwave on high for 1 to 1 1/2 minutes, until mixture is blended. With electric mixer or whisk, beat eggs until frothy. Add sugar, chocolate mixture, and vanilla. Blend flour with baking powder. Whisk into chocolate mixture. Fold in pecans and chocolate morsels. Pour into an 8 or 9-inch, glass pie plate. Microwave on high for 6 minutes, turning every 2 minutes. Mixture will be soft, but will firm as it cools. Allow to cool for 1 hour before cutting.

Serves: Makes 20 brownies

HOMESTYLE ALMOND CUSTARD

Ingredients:

2 cups whole milk
2 eggs
1/4 cup sugar
1 teaspoon almond
  extract
1/4 teaspoon cinnamon
2 tablespoons slivered
  almonds, toasted

Directions:

Pour milk into a 1-quart microwave mixing bowl. Cover and microwave on high for 4 minutes. Milk will be frothy and scalded. Do not boil milk. Beat eggs well and add sugar, and almond extract. Pour in hot milk. Pour about 3/4 cup mixture into each of 4 glass or microwave custard cups. Place on a round microwave tray, cover, and microwave on medium for 8 to 10 minutes. The custard will be just set. Sprinkle with cinnamon and slivered almonds. Allow to rest for 30 minutes before serving.

Serves: 4

HOT AND SPICY RASPBERRY FLAMBÉ

Ingredients:

1/2 cup sugar
1 tablespoon arrowroot
1/2 teaspoon cinnamon
1/4 teaspoon nutmeg
1/2 teaspoon allspice
1/4 cup water
Juice of 1 lemon (2
  tablespoons)
2 cups raspberries (fresh
  or dry pack frozen)
1 pint vanilla or
  chocolate ice cream
1/2 cup nut liqueur

Directions:

In a 1-quart, glass microwave dish, blend sugar, arrowroot, cinnamon, nutmeg, and allspice. Whisk in 1/4 cup water and lemon juice. Whisk until mixture is smooth. Cover and microwave on high until mixture comes to a boil, about 2 1/2 minutes. Whisk to remove any lumps. Rinse and drain raspberries. Stir into hot sauce. Cover and microwave on high for 2 minutes or until mixture boils. Scoop ice cream into heat proof sherbet glasses. Freeze. When ready to serve, pour liqueur into a glass custard cup. Microwave on low for 30 seconds. Add to raspberry sauce, ignite carefully, and carefully ladle over ice cream.

Serves: 4

OLD FASHIONED BAKED APPLES

Ingredients:

6 large baking apples, such as Rome, Jonathan or Granny Smith
3/4 cup raisins
1/2 cup brown sugar, packed
1 tablespoon butter
1/2 teaspoon ground cinnamon
1/2 teaspoon ground nutmeg
1/2 cup water
1 cup half-and-half

Directions:

Core apples with a wide corer. Make a collar around each apple by cutting a strip of peel from around the top of each apple. Place apples in a round 2-quart microwave casserole or microwave ring mold. Fill apples with raisins. In a 1-quart microwave bowl, place brown sugar, butter, cinnamon, nutmeg, and 1/2 cup water. Cover and microwave on high for 1 minute, 30 seconds. Sugar should be melted, and mixture very hot. Pour hot sugar over and around apples. Cover and microwave on high for 10 to 12 minutes. Turn dish 1/4 turn every 3 minutes. Apples will be hot and very tender. Remove apples to individual serving dishes. Serve with half-and-half.

Serves: 6

MICROWAVE CAPPUCCINO

Ingredients:

1 cup vanilla ice cream
4 microwave proof wine glasses (or microwave proof Irish coffee glasses), 8 ounces each
4 cups Italian expresso coffee (regular or decaffeinated), brewed in a drip coffee maker

Directions:

Scoop 1/4 cup ice cream into each glass. Microwave until ice cream is warm and bubbled up into the cup, 1 1/2 to 2 minutes (for all 4 glasses). Add brewed espresso.

Serves: 4

PEANUT BRITTLE

Ingredients:

1 cup brown sugar, packed

1/2 cup dark corn syrup

2 cups dry roasted, unsalted peanuts

1 teaspoon butter

1 teaspoon vanilla

1 teaspoon baking soda

Directions:

Grease a 10 x 14 jellyroll pan. In a 2-quart microwave bowl, combine brown sugar with dark corn syrup. Cover and microwave on high for 4 minutes. Stir in peanuts, cover and microwave on high for 3 minutes. Stir in butter and vanilla, cover and microwave on high for 2 minutes. At this point, test candy by dropping a small amount into very cold water. Candy should be at hard boil stage, meaning a small amount will form hard and brittle strings when dropped into very cold water. This will also register 300° on a candy thermometer or on a microwave probe. Blend in baking soda and stir until mixture is light and foamy. Pour candy onto jellyroll pan, spreading to edges as much as possible. As candy cools, stretch into thin sheets using palms of hands that have been buttered. Cool completely, then break into pieces.

Serves: Makes 1 pound

HOT LEMONADE

Ingredients:

4 lemons, squeezed (about 1/2 cup fresh lemon juice)

1 cup water

1/3 cup honey

2 ounces whiskey

Directions:

In a 1-quart microwave dish, combine lemon juice with water and honey. Microwave on high for 5 minutes. Mixture will be near a boil. Stir to blend honey. Pour into 2 heated microwave proof mugs. Put 1 ounce whiskey in each mug. Serve immediately.

Serves: 2

QUICK BANANAS FOSTER

Ingredients:

1 pint good quality vanilla or coffee-flavored ice cream

4 small bananas, firm but ripe

2 tablespoons butter, melted

2 tablespoons brown sugar, firmly packed

1/4 teaspoon cinnamon

1 tablespoon banana (or other) liqueur

1/2 cup dark rum

Directions:

In advance, place 1 scoop of ice cream in 4 wide-mouthed, heat proof champagne or dessert glasses. Freeze until serving time. Peel and slice bananas. Place butter in a 1-quart microwave dish. Add bananas and turn to coat all sides with butter. Cover and microwave on high for 1 minute. Bananas will be golden and very soft. Sprinkle with brown sugar and cinnamon. Cover and microwave for an additional 90 seconds until sugar melts and blends with butter. When ready to serve add liqueur and rum to banana mixture. Light carefully. When aflame, carefully ladle over frozen ice cream.

Serves: 4

S'MORES

Ingredients:

1 cup chocolate morsels or chunks

1 (14 ounce) can sweetened condensed milk (not evaporated milk)

1 teaspoon vanilla extract

2 cups miniature marshmallows

32 graham crackers

Directions:

In a 1-quart microwave dish, combine chocolate morsels, milk, and vanilla. Cover and microwave on high for 2 to 3 minutes until chocolate melts. Do not overcook. Make 1 S'MORE at a time in the following manner: spread 1 tablespoon chocolate sauce onto a graham cracker; top with marshamallows and a second graham cracker spread with 1 tablespoon chocolate sauce, chocolate sauce side down. Wrap in plastic wrap until ready to serve. *To serve:* place S'MORE on a napkin and microwave on high for 15 seconds or until marshmallows just start to melt. Remove plastic wrapping and serve.

Serves: Makes 16

INDEX

Desserts and Beverages